Gender and Classroom Interaction

A RESEAR ...

Christine Howe

The Scottish Council for Research in Education

SCRE Publication 138
Using Research Series 19 (*formerly* Practitioner MiniPaper Series)

Series editors: Wynne Harlen
                 Rosemary Wake

Published 1997

ISBN 1 86003 034 3

Copyright © 1997 The Scottish Council for Research in Education

Cover photograph: Simon Saffery
Grateful thanks to pupils at Gracemount Primary School, Edinburgh

Design and typesetting by SCRE Information Services.

Printed and bound in Great Britain for the Scottish Council for Research in Education, 15 St John Street, Edinburgh EH8 8JR, by Macdonald Lindsay Pindar, Edgefield Road, Loanhead, Midlothian.

Acknowledgements

This book evolved from a report into gender differences in classroom interaction which was commissioned by the Scottish Office Education and Industry Department. Thanks are therefore due to SOEID for providing the opportunity to review and reflect on the relevant body of research. Thanks are also due to the staff of the Centre for Research into Interactive Learning for their tolerance of the 'time-out' from normal duties that preparing the report involved, and to Andrew Noble for his help in unearthing references, preparing summaries and generating ideas. The transformation of the report into a book was helped enormously by the comments of Rosemary Wake from the Scottish Council for Research in Education together with one anonymous referee. Thus, finally, thanks are also due to these two individuals.

Contents

1
Theory and Practice

"Do schools perpetuate behavioural differences between males and females? Does classroom interaction reflect the gender divisions in society, and more than that does it also contribute to their continuation? "

Schools, according to Delamont, 'develop and reinforce sex segregations, stereotypes and even discriminations which exaggerate the negative aspects of sex roles in the outside world, when they could be trying to alleviate them' (1990, p2). It is somewhat strange to find Delamont writing about *sex* segregations and *sex* roles: most contemporary theorists use the term 'gender' for the behavioural differences between males and females. Delamont acknowledges this herself a few pages later, and admits that she was referring to 'sex' to add force to her point. She certainly succeeds for the reader is left in no doubt as to what is being claimed: schools are active agents in perpetuating the behavioural differences between males and females. Thus the appetite is whetted for the substance of the book, which turns out to be Delamont's complex and multi-faceted view of how perpetuation proceeds.

Many factors are discussed but one in particular seems central to the argument, the social interaction which occurs in classrooms. Is this correct? Do schools perpetuate behavioural differences between males and females? Does classroom interaction reflect the gender divisions in society, and more than that, does it also contribute to their continuation? The aim of the present book is to find out what can be concluded from existing research, and to make proposals relating to further action.

However, before proceeding, it would seem advisable to take a preliminary step, and specify the ways in which classroom interaction might *in theory* result in discrimination. After all, it will otherwise be virtually impossible to pinpoint what is significant

1

within the research and what is tangential. This, therefore, is how this introductory chapter begins. Then having established a theoretical framework, the chapter will provide a brief overview of the book's main substance.

Possible roles for classroom interaction

Gender divisions in society have of course changed in the recent past, and there is every likelihood that they will continue to change. To take just one example, the percentage of adult women definable as 'economically active' (that is in paid employment or officially unemployed) remained at around 33% for the first 60 years of this century (Webb, M, 1989). Since then, it has steadily risen to its current level of 50%, meaning that for every two women who were economically active in the mid-1960s three are economically active now. Nevertheless within this context of change there are many constancies. Even at 50%, the percentage of women who are economically active is nowhere near as high as the percentage of men, and there has always been a gap between the two figures. Furthermore, the average earnings of women who are in full-time employment have never risen above 75% of the average earnings of their male equivalents, a difference which is attributable to two main factors. The first is the concentration of women in a number of traditionally low-paid occupations, for example clerical work, hairdressing and professional care, and the second is the relative failure of women to climb in occupational hierarchies, and so to be under-represented in promoted posts in teaching or in managerial positions in industry. In addition though, there is the fact that nine out of every ten part-time workers are women. Since the percentage of women workers in part-time employment is closely related to the age of the youngest child, this tendency can undoubtedly be attributed to a further constancy in gender divisions, the higher prioritising of domestic responsibilities by women when compared with men.

Thus gender divisions exist in the choice of occupational sectors, in the standing and influence within sectors, and in the prioritising of the occupational relative to the domestic. The question which this book will be geared towards addressing is, then, whether classroom interaction could be contributing to any or all of these three points of difference. Starting with the choice of occupational sectors, the issue would appear straightforward: does classroom interaction create conditions where pupils of one sex or the other come to believe that they are unsuited to certain occupations and/or the school subjects required for them? For instance, does classroom interaction give boys the idea that they are unsuited to clerical work and/or the 'office and information studies' classes that might seem to be relevant? Does it give girls corresponding views about careers as technicians or mechanics and/or of 'technical studies' as a school subject? The answer to such questions might be yes in any one of several circumstances. The first would be if classroom interaction leads boys and girls to perform differently in different subjects, providing them with objective evidence of contrasting suitabilities. This would amount to interaction exerting a direct influence upon academic achievement and, by way of this, an indirect influence on occupational choice. The possibility that this might be so would certainly be acknowledged by followers of the Russian psychologist Lev Vygotsky, for a central tenet of the Vygotskyan canon is that social interaction plays a key role in the determination of learning (see, for example, Newman & Holzman, 1993). Thus subsequent chapters will pay careful attention to the potential influence of classroom interaction upon academic achievement.

In addition though, and regardless of the implications for academic achievement, classroom interaction may affect perceptions of occupational suitability by making pupils of one sex or the other feel uncomfortable with certain occupations and/or associated subjects. Statements which seem likely to have this effect abound in the literature, including the following from a male teacher of science: 'One thing I hate and detest is ignorant females and this school is lousy with them these days. Suppose I'd better address myself to you lads. Don't want to see that ugly lot in my lab' (quoted by Delamont (1990, p58, from the doctoral research of Gillborn). Unfortunately, it would be difficult to study such statements systematically: their 'political incorrectness' means that they are unlikely to be displayed on any wide scale when researchers are present. Hence, they will not be considered in the main body of this book. This said, it is possible for interactive experiences to make individuals feel uncomfortable, even if they are not explicitly told that their presence is unwelcome, and such experiences will be carefully considered.

Moving to standing and influence within occupational sectors, this is obviously several degrees removed from what happens in schools. Nevertheless, classroom interaction could still be relevant. To achieve positions of influence within the work context (and to use these positions effectively once they have been achieved), it is usually necessary to display one's problem-solving and managerial skills on a fairly public stage. It is necessary in other words to speak out in meetings and to debate in front of an audience. The classroom is not the workplace but it is still a public forum. The possibility has therefore to be recognised that classroom interaction might provide boys and girls with different opportunities to acquire and practise the relevant skills. From points made already about who has power and influence in the world of work, the opportunities would, to be relevant, have to favour boys.

With these considerations in mind, the research into classroom interaction will be scrutinised to establish whether gender differences relevant to public display do exist. To the extent that they do, a further question follows, namely how do members of the 'non-displaying' sex respond? Do they withdraw altogether, in which case adverse consequences for learning might be expected, or do they adopt compensatory strategies of a more private nature? Do they, for example, approach the teacher individually in private study periods? If it is the latter, academic achievement might be preserved but there might be implications for interpersonal relations, in particular a growing empathy with relations of a private, individualised nature rather than a public one.

These implications are interesting because they could in theory be relevant to the third source of gender divisions signalled above, the difference in value attached to domestic and occupational roles, for the domestic clearly carries a private, individualised dimension. Hence, these possibilities too will be addressed within the book. The question will be asked as to whether classroom interaction could result in gender differences in public and private learning. If it could, the further issue will be raised of whether this could be significant for subsequent career paths towards employment or the home.

The structure of the book

As the book progresses, considerable evidence will be unearthed to show that gender differences do exist in classroom interaction, and that these differences are linkable with choices of occupational sectors, with standing and influence within sectors, and with occupational versus domestic prioritising. However, while this is important, it should be noted that the linkages between interaction and outcome are, at present, mainly hypothetical. Virtually all of the classroom interaction research is limited to descriptions of what takes place. Very few studies have related interaction to the measures of academic performance or social attitude that would be needed to support statements about longer term consequences. This limitation is of course significant when the book addresses its second major concern, the implications for action. Action in terms of further research is most definitely warranted, but action in terms of practical intervention seems open to debate. On the one hand, it may be argued that intervention should await the results of the further research; on the other, it may be felt that a generation of pupils should not be 'sacrificed' when links between classroom interaction and roles in society are already presumable if not proved. The pros and cons here will be briefly discussed, with the arguments being deemed, albeit tentatively, to point towards practical intervention now rather than later.

The implications for further research and practical intervention are considered in the book's final chapter. To reach that point, the book proceeds through four substantive chapters which are organised around contrasting contexts where interaction takes place, namely whole-class discussion, desk-based group work, group work around computers, and discussion for oral assessment. In each chapter, an attempt is made to synthesise the research that currently exists, appraise it critically, and to see how it can be related to divisions in society. In line with customary practice the term 'gender' will be used when discussing behavioural distinctions and 'sex' will be restricted to the non-behavioural. Without doubt, it would have been possible to organise the material in ways other than the one selected. It would for example have been feasible to work around divisions between the primary and secondary sectors, or between the major school subjects. However, such divisions would have served to put interaction somewhat in the background. It seemed preferable to keep the focus on what is, after all, the book's major concern by using interaction as the organising principle. This is not to say that sector and school subject will be ignored. On the contrary, they will be referred to throughout, but it is to say that reference will be within a framework which centres on the key situations where interaction takes place.

2
Whole-Class Interaction

"All in all then, the research suggests that pupils play an active part in bringing the gender differences in classroom interaction into being: boys are more likely than girls to create conditions where their contributions will be sought by teachers, and they are more likely than girls to push themselves forward when contributors are not explicitly selected."

To put the research on gender differences in whole-class interaction into context, it is necessary to look briefly at the wider body of research into whole-class interaction. This research gained momentum in the late 1960s, no doubt in response to the belief which was then emerging that the educational process is as important a focus as the learning outcome. At first, the research used rather crude methods, adapted in fact from the methods used by early social psychologists. These typically involved observing behaviour and coding it *in situ* into a small number of global categories, such as 'praise' and 'response'. Inevitably, the conclusions drawn were somewhat general, being limited to broad quantitative statements. Nevertheless, one set of such statements had an appealing resonance in its day, and has never been seriously challenged by subsequent research. This is Flanders' (1970) famous 'two-thirds rule', that: (a) for about two-thirds of the time someone is talking, (b) about two-thirds of this talk is the teacher's, and (c) about two-thirds of the teacher's talk consists of 'lecturing' or 'asking questions'.

Unpacking Flanders' rule, it seems clear that a great deal of classroom talk is non-interactive, being limited via lecturing to what Barnes (1973) calls the 'transmissive' mode. However, the occurrence of asking questions suggests some interactive behaviour, but interactive behaviour which is very much teacher-led. This impression is confirmed by the research of Sinclair & Coulthard (1975), which demonstrates, firstly, that whole-class interaction typically follows an initiation-response-feedback structure and,

7

secondly, that responsibility for initiation and feedback lies almost exclusively with teachers. Commenting on Sinclair & Coulthard's work some years later, Edwards & Mercer (1987) attest to the continuing truth of its claims. The basic exchange structure is, they point out, 'once seen, impossible to ignore in any observed classroom talk' (p9). Accepting then that the characteristic pattern of whole-class interaction is teacher initiation, pupil response and teacher feedback, the crucial issues as regards gender would appear to be as follows: (a) can gender differences be detected in the patterning of pupils' responses, (b) if so, can the differences be related back to teacher initiations, and (c) does teacher feedback vary according to gender? Since the early 1970s there has been a steady flow of studies concerned with one or more of these issues, and these studies are the focus of this chapter. After a brief sketch of the methodology, the results will be summarised as they bear on the issues, and then placed in the broader context of divisions in society.

The main conclusions are:

■ Boys contribute more than girls to whole-class interaction, and they receive more feedback from teachers on what they contribute.

■ The predominance of boys is partly, though not entirely, due to teachers selecting boys to contribute more frequently than they do girls.

■ The differences are unlikely to have relevance to academic performance, but may exert an influence on learning strategy, public confidence and ultimately gender divisions.

Methodological background

The relevant studies have been conducted in Australasia, the United States and Great Britain, although none of the British studies has been located in Scotland. Without doubt, the most comprehensive studies took place in the first two locations. For example, while the number of teachers/classrooms featuring in the Australasian and American investigations is seldom below 20 per study and reaches up to 60, the British samples rarely attain double figures. Often, it is a question of small case-studies in one or two classrooms. This said, the British results do concur with the results from elsewhere and because of this we can probably accept them, although it would be reassuring to have a comprehensive UK study, particularly one located in Scotland. Certainly, the UK studies, like the studies elsewhere in the world, have covered all age bands, from five to 17. Unfortunately, however, they also suffer from a limitation which applies worldwide. This is that while the work with primary school pupils typically covers the full range of activities, work with secondary school pupils emphasises mathematics and science.

In terms of data collection, virtually all of the studies used direct observation in ordinary classrooms. However, there was a shift in the mid-1980s in the observational techniques favoured. Before then, the techniques were in line with the generality of whole-class research, emphasising as already said, the *in situ* categorisation of behaviour. Often the categories were derived from previous whole-class research which lacked a gender focus. For example, Stake & Katz' (1982) work on the interplay of teacher and pupil gender in determining interaction used a categorisation scheme that was based on Flanders (1970). Since the mid-1980s, most research has involved tape-recording, either video or audio. Moreover, when *in situ* coding has been preserved (as for example in work conducted in New Zealand by Smith & Glynn, 1990), it has become associated with extremely rigorous methods of data collection. This said, the potential for fine-grained analysis that methodological advances allow has not been fully exploited. There has been a tendency to perpetuate the global categories that *in situ* coding necessitated, almost as if established practices have evolved their own momentum.

Gender differences in whole-class interaction

In view of the issues identified earlier as of particular concern, the results of the studies are presented with reference first to pupils' responses, then to teachers' initiations, and finally to teachers' feedback. Starting then with responses, there can be little doubt that gender differences pervade the whole-class context. The most straightforward manifestation of this lies in the sheer volume of contributions, with boys being shown, repeatedly, to have a disproportionate share of the floor. Evidence for this can be found in three British studies: French & French (1984) with ten- to eleven-year olds, Bousted (1989) with 15-year olds, and Swann & Graddol

(1988) with nine- to eleven-year olds; and one Australian study: Dart & Clarke (1988) with 14-year olds. Importantly, the gender differences do not result from behaviour which is consistent across all the boys in a class. Rather, the studies show repeatedly that they stem from the extreme talkativeness of a subgroup. This ties in with research by Jones & Gerig (1994) which focuses exclusively on 'silent students' and which shows that silence during whole-class discussion was characteristic of boys as well as of girls.

Of course, accepting that some boys (albeit not all) contribute extensively is not the same as accepting that the contributions made by these boys are in any way superior. Quantity does not after all guarantee quality, and it is therefore unfortunate that a relatively small number of studies have used the content-based analyses that would provide information about this. This relates, without doubt, to the reliance on global coding categories already highlighted. Nevertheless, from the research that currently exists, it would be hard to deny qualitative as well as quantitative superiority to those boys who contribute. Dart & Clarke (1988) show that boys' contributions dominate regardless of whether the discussion concerns school subject content, classroom management or pupil behaviour. Good, Sikes & Brophy (1973) and Swann & Graddol (1988) indicate that extended explanations are more likely to come from boys, with girls' contributions often being limited to simple statements of fact. Indeed, moving away from purely verbal responses, a large-scale American study by Jones & Wheatley (1989), involving 60 teachers and over 1,300 pupils, demonstrates that boys are more likely than girls to conduct demonstrations in science classes.

It has already been pointed out that what pupils say during whole-class interactions is seldom initiated by them. Rather, it is typically in response to initiations from teachers, these often being in the form of questions. Recognising this, boys must be responding to their teachers to a disproportionately high extent, but how does this come about? It is possible to call on a mixture of British and American studies for clarification, and their message is a situation of surprising complexity. Certainly there is evidence, for example in the study by Swann & Graddol (1988), that boys are favoured when teachers come to choose pupils to answer their questions.

However, the same study also shows boys 'chipping in' more than girls in a relatively informal classroom where pupils were not explicitly selected, a finding that has been confirmed by Bousted (1989) and Sadker & Sadker (1985). The latter found boys eight times more likely than girls to call out in class.

In addition though, there is evidence that boys make themselves relatively prominent, suggesting that teachers' choices may be a reflection of 'visibility' rather than gender *per se*. The most obvious manifestation of this lies in hand-raising: Swann & Graddol (1988) found that teachers tend to select the pupil whose hand goes up first, and this pupil is very likely to be a boy. However, boys are also likely to be the focus of attention even before the questions are asked. Boys have been shown by Good *et al.* (1973) and Morgan & Dunn (1988) to be more restless than girls in classrooms, and their movement may attract attention. In addition, they have been found by Morgan & Dunn and by Good, Cooper & Blakely (1980) to misbehave more than girls, and teachers may be monitoring where misbehaviour is anticipated. Certainly, teachers gaze more at boys: referring once more to the study by Swann & Graddol, boys were gazed at by their teachers approximately twice as often as girls.

All in all, then, the research suggests that pupils play an active part in bringing the gender differences in classroom interaction into being: boys are more likely than girls to create conditions where their contributions will be sought by teachers, and they are more likely than girls to push themselves forward when contributors are not explicitly selected. However, this is not to say that teachers are entirely passive in the process. Morgan & Dunn (1988) found high levels of contribution being described by teachers as 'showing off' when they came from girls but 'interest' when they came from boys. If this is communicated (albeit subtly) to pupils, it could have longer-term implications for visibility and for volunteering. Unfortunately, Morgan & Dunn did not explore this possibility explicitly, and thus the point is merely speculative. In any event, this study involved four classrooms only and was restricted to the youngest age groups.

Given that boys respond more than girls whether or not they are selected, it seems likely that boys will receive more teacher feedback, and this is confirmed, for American pupils at least, by both Good *et al.* (1973) and Jones & Wheatley (1989). However, gender differences in the overall volume of feedback do not necessarily mean gender differences in all aspects of its content, and more detailed analyses are required to look at this. In fact, a number of studies have attempted such analyses, many focusing on the relative frequency of positive remarks such as 'You're absolutely right' and 'What a great idea' and negative remarks like 'For the five hundredth time, seven times eight is not 58' and 'No, no, it's not about transport; it's about.....?'. The message from the studies is not entirely consistent here. Good *et al.*, Jones & Wheatley and Simpson & Erickson (1983) find more positive remarks being directed at boys, but Stake & Katz (1982) find no gender differences. All four of these studies document higher levels of negative feedback to boys than to girls, a finding which is consistently attributed to male misbehaviour. However, Smith & Glynn (1990) find no gender differences in what they call 'criticism'.

It is unclear at present how the deviant results should be interpreted, whether for instance they should be dismissed as freaks of sampling or whether they should hint at factors in addition gender which are relevant to feedback. It is hard to find additional factors which differentiate Stake & Katz (1982) from the other studies which bear on positive feedback. All the studies are American, they overlap with regard to age group, school subject and observational technique, and they all include male and female teachers. Looking at the studies which are relevant to negative feedback, Smith & Glynn (1990) does stand out a little. Reflecting arguably the New Zealand context in which it was conducted, the study documents unusually high levels of teacher control over classroom activities. This resulted in criticism being rare in absolute terms (and in relation to the other studies) regardless of gender. An implication is, then, that control levels need to be considered along with gender. Nevertheless, the message remains: in general boys receive more negative feedback than girls, and probably more positive feedback as well. The only further qualification, and it is minor, comes from Good *et al.* (1973) who endorse the findings relating to both positive and negative feedback when looking at the absolute number of remarks but find that the ratio of negative to positive remarks is greater for boys than for girls. In terms of impact on pupils, the proportion of negative and positive feedback may be as significant as the absolute amounts.

Whole-class research in a broader context

Summing up then, the studies undoubtedly provide evidence that there are gender differences in how pupils contribute to whole-class interactions, these differences amounting to the quantitative and qualitative dominance of contributions from boys. The differences may be influenced by strategies initiated by the teacher, but they are at least as likely to reflect the visibility and/or self-promotion of boys. Furthermore, because boys contribute more, they receive more feedback, and this may apply to both positive and negative reactions. With the exception of the inconsistencies just noted, the studies are in agreement, despite being conducted in three distinct parts of the world, with a wide age range, and up to 20 years apart. In relation to this last point, it is sobering to discover how little has changed between the early 1970s and the present time.

By and large, the studies also concur with each other regardless of the sex of the teacher. The sex of the teacher does have an impact on classroom interaction: Stake & Katz (1982) find male teachers using more blunt negatives ('No, that's wrong') and female teachers offering more encouragement and sympathy. However, there is little evidence of boys and girls being treated *differently* by male or female teachers, with Whyte's (1984) analysis of secondary school science lessons being the only apparent exception. White's analysis was based on observations made during the Girls into Science and Technology project, a project aimed to help teachers devise interactive strategies which would improve girls' attitudes to science and increase their participation. A small group of the teachers involved in the project managed to achieve classroom interactions that were evenly balanced between boys and girls, and relative to their numbers in the overall sample, female teachers were over-represented within this group. Nevertheless, apart from Whyte's study, there are few indications that the sex of the teacher makes a substantive difference, and indeed there are few indications that teacher variables of any description exert much influence.

Pupil variables may be more relevant, particularly ability: Good *et al.* (1973) and, more elliptically, Morgan & Dunn (1988) suggest that high-ability boys are particularly favoured while low-ability boys can sometimes contribute the least of all. This may be significant when trying to interpret the finding reported earlier that the dominance of boys reflects the talkativeness of a subgroup.

In general then, the results seem very much of a piece, but is it a piece with wider significance? Before attempting an answer, it is important to note that the research suffers from two shortcomings which restrict what can be said. First, there is the fact already highlighted that the studies based in secondary schools have emphasised mathematics and science, and there is no guarantee that the same results would have been obtained in the humanities or the social sciences. Perhaps though, generalisability is a reasonable working assumption. The findings from secondary schools concur with the primary, and these were obtained for the full range of curriculum subjects. In addition, a few secondary school studies (albeit a very few) included the humanities and the social sciences, and their results fit the overall picture.

Moving to the second limitation, this stems from the fact that, relative to the other interactive contexts to be discussed in the book, the whole-class research is the most extreme example of a problem signalled earlier, namely the tendency to emphasise description at the expense of outcome. Indeed as regards whole-class interaction, we know nothing about the implications for either academic performance or social attitudes. Probably, the only thing to be said regarding the academic dimension is that if we assume that the secondary results apply generally and are not restricted to maths and science, we can probably also assume that they do not have straightforward implications for achievement. Recent surveys such as Powney (1996) have shown that when grades are averaged across school subjects, girls perform similarly and perhaps slightly better than boys in public examinations. The reverse would seem to be predicted given a straightforward relation between whole-class interaction and academic achievement.

Accepting the implausibility of a straightforward relation between whole-class interaction and academic achievement, there is, however, the possibility of a more indirect association. It is after all possible that the gender divisions lead girls to adopt alternative and seemingly effective 'compensatory strategies' which ensure that their needs are met, and which impact on the learning process and not on its outcome. Interestingly, there are hints in one or two of the studies that compensatory strategies may in fact be adopted: both Good *et al.* (1980) and Dart & Clarke (1988) report girls making individual approaches to teachers more often than boys, and Jones & Gerig (1994) find that by virtue of these approaches girls' questions are more likely than boys' to be answered. These hints should certainly be followed up in subsequent research, and maybe not just from the academic perspective.

It will not have escaped attention that if boys are prominent in the whole-class arena while girls operate one-to-one, then evidence is already emerging that the learning of boys is a more public process than the learning of girls. Certainly, Taber (1992) makes precisely this point. However, earlier it was argued that being valued within the public domain in school may be relevant to achieving influence within the work context and indeed for seeing the work context as a significant place to be. It may be, then, that the whole-class experience of boys has relevance to these aspects of the male role in society. By the same token, it may also be that the whole-class experience of girls has relevance to the female role in society, leading girls not only to shun status and influence within the public domain of work but also to feel comfortable with more private, individualised encounters.

Obviously, all this is pure speculation, being far removed from what the work has shown. Nevertheless, it is worth raising at this early stage to signal a possibly significant line to follow. It will certainly be revisited in the chapters to follow. However, to sum up for the present, the following points can now be said to have emerged:

- On average, boys contribute more to whole-class interaction than girls, regardless of whether we look at the number of utterances or the quality of their content.
- The predominance of boys' contributions stems from the extreme talkativeness of a subgroup.
- Teachers select boys to contribute more often than girls, in part at least because boys attract their attention more in whole-class contexts.
- Boys receive more feedback on their contributions, both positive and negative, although a greater percentage of their feedback is negative when compared with girls'.

■ Teacher characteristics, including sex, have no significant bearing upon these findings.

■ The results are unlikely to bear directly upon academic performance, although they may have relevance to the learning strategies pupils adopt.

■ The putatively more 'public' strategy of boys and the putatively more 'private' strategy of girls may have consequences for gender divisions, but no research of relevance is currently available.

3
Desk-Based Group Work

"It is clear that principles of effective group work are beginning to emerge, and sooner or later these seem likely to exert an influence upon classroom practice. This unfortunately complicates the situation enormously as regards the gender dimension."

The previous chapter showed how the work on gender could be related to, and was to some extent part of, the wider context of research into whole-class interaction in general. In introducing the wider context, mention was made of Flanders' (1970) two-thirds rule which stated, amongst other things, that in classrooms two-thirds of the talk comes from teachers. By the same token, one-third of the talk comes from pupils, and from the previous section it will be clear that much of this one-third will be in response to teachers. This leaves precious little talk between the pupils themselves, and yet such talk has been advocated via an emphasis on group collaboration in virtually all British curricular documents of the past 30 years. It was one of the strongest messages in Plowden (1967), and it has been preserved in both the National Curriculum for England and Wales and the 5-14 Programme for Scotland. Within the 5-14 Programme, the English language guidelines present 'talking and listening in groups' as major curricula strands (SOED, 1991) and the mathematics guidelines refer explicitly to the need for pupils to exchange ideas while engaging in problem solving (SOED, 1993).

If Flanders' rule still has relevance (and we have already seen that it probably does), the implication is that the advocacy of group work in policy documents has fallen on deaf ears. When pupils talk, it is to teachers and not to each other; and in any event pupil talk is the exception rather than the rule. What then has happened? A large-scale study of eight- to eleven-year olds by Galton, Simon & Croll (1980) provides what is almost certainly still the correct answer.

Galton *et al.* found that pupils at this age level sit at desks which are arranged in groups for most of the day, but for the bulk of the time they work as individuals on their own tasks. Despite the group-based seating arrangement, it is quite exceptional to find pupils working collaboratively. Moreover, on the rare occasions that this happens, talk is minimal. Boydell (1975) found that the average length of conversations during group work was less than 25 seconds, and Bennett, Desforges, Cockburn & Wilkinson (1984) report that when such conversations occur they can seldom be regarded as adding to the quality of the task. Insofar as they do relate to the task (and they are quite likely to focus on last night's television or this evening's activities), they are typically limited to how much has been completed and/or on how resource materials should be shared.

Faced with this dismal situation, one possibility is to place less emphasis on group work in British classrooms. However, this is not the only option. An alternative is to argue that even if group work is not working effectively in its current form, there may be other methods of organisation which achieve greater success. Because group work has always seemed desirable on social grounds, the quest for such different methods has been high on the research agenda for the past ten years. A variety of strands have been followed, the most significant probably being those relating to division of roles, style of interaction, task design and external incentives. It would be inappropriate here to attempt a thorough review of what has emerged, but a few points are necessary to set the scene for the subsequent analysis of gender. These will be covered in the next section. Thereafter, material on gender differences will be presented using much the same structure as the previous chapter and, it must be admitted, leading to parallel conclusions. In particular:

■ Boys occupy 'centre-stage' in group work, being seen as the primary source of help by both boys and girls.

■ This may not have serious implications for academic achievement at present but it could do so in the future.

Getting the best from group work

Starting with work relating to the division of roles in groups, the central issue has been the desirability of what is called 'symmetry' in the composition of groups. Within symmetric groups, all pupils are given equal responsibility for ensuring success. Within asymmetric groups, some pupils are instructed to help the others, as for example in so-called 'peer tutoring'. The symmetry versus asymmetry issue is closely related to the question of the distribution of ability and/or knowledge but it is not identical. For one thing, it is possible to have differing levels of ability/knowledge and yet equal responsibility and hence symmetric roles. To date, the main message from the research (see, for example, Damon & Phelps, 1989; Rogoff, 1990) is that symmetric roles are preferable when the content of the learning task is conceptual. Furthermore, it does not matter whether levels of ability/knowledge are similar or different. However, asymmetric roles are better when the emphasis is on skills; and when roles are asymmetric it is preferable to have more able pupils doing the helping.

Moving to styles of interaction, two issues have dominated: (a) whether pupils should work collaboratively throughout the task or whether they should undertake separate parts of the 'jigsaw' which they pool collaboratively at the end and (b) whether the mode of interaction should be co-operative or competitive. Surprisingly, there are no studies making direct comparisons between full and partial collaboration. However, as Damon & Phelps (1989) point out, the interaction achievable during collaboration has been shown repeatedly to have beneficial consequences, and this surely implies that it should not be diluted into the partial version. In addition, Damon & Phelps show that separate activities can foster competition between group members, and returning to the second issue there is conclusive evidence (see, for example Johnson & Johnson, 1995) that co-operative interaction is superior to competitive.

As regards task design, there is consensus over the need for a high level of structure (see, for example, Gillies & Ashman, 1994). Indeed the lack of structure in routine classroom activities has been identified as a major reason for the problems with desk-based group work that were identified at the start of this chapter. However, a great deal remains to be established about how tasks should be organised, granted a high level of structure. Strathclyde University research relating to conceptual knowledge in science (Howe, Tolmie, Greer & Mackenzie, 1995; Tolmie, Howe, Mackenzie & Greer, 1993) has shown, for instance, that tiny variants on a predict outcome – test prediction – interpret results format, have major implications for both group interaction and subsequent learning. It matters substantially, for example, whether pupils produce their own interpretations of why things float or sink or why they cool down quickly or slowly, as opposed to selecting from a list produced by the teacher. The former is considerably more effective! Research is only just beginning here but it is unlikely that such results will turn out to be isolated examples once the issue of task structure is explored systematically.

Looking finally at external incentives, the debate here hangs around the need to assign grades to group performance. Slavin (1995) reiterates a line that he has been taking for some considerable time, that learning may take place without grades in the rarefied atmosphere of a research project but this will not happen in the run-of-the-mill context of a standard classroom. The jury is still out here, but two points from Strathclyde research are probably worth noting. Firstly, Smith, Howe & Low (1995) have obtained promising results with a group-based mathematics project which ran in ordinary classrooms over a full school term and made no use whatsoever of external incentives. Secondly, Howe, Rodgers & Tolmie (1990) and Howe, Tolmie & Rodgers (1992) have found that pupils can benefit academically from collaborating even when group performance is poor. This is because group interaction can act as a catalyst for subsequent reflection and learning, regardless of the quality of the interaction itself. However, this catalysing effect would probably not have happened if (in contrast to Howe *et al.*'s practice) the poor group performance had been fed back to the pupils in the form of grades, for why should they have thought about the implications of something that they knew to be poor?

Implications for the study of gender

Without doubt a great deal remains to be done. Nevertheless, it is clear that principles of effective group work are beginning to emerge, and sooner or later these seem likely to exert an influence upon classroom practice. This unfortunately complicates the situation enormously as regards the gender dimension. On the one hand, it seems desirable to consider the gender implications of the situation that currently exists, for these are the only ones that could possibly relate to present divisions in society. However, the present situation will probably change, meaning that the conclusions which are drawn could soon become outmoded. Thus on the other hand, it also seems necessary to explore whether the research sketched in the previous section has unearthed gender effects. The trouble is that if it has, these effects will at best be relatable to gender divisions in some future world, and at worst be relatable to nothing. After all, even though much of the research has been done in classrooms rather than laboratories, it is still experimental, and whatever we may think about the details of Slavin's (1995) argument about external incentives, he is surely correct to warn us, as noted above, that effects obtained during experiments cannot be relied on to apply more generally.

On the face of it, the best strategy might seem to be to consider both the current situation and the possible future. However, this will not be the strategy adopted here for one simple reason, the existence of contradictions within the material relating to the current situation. Take for example the three studies mentioned earlier, that is Boydell (1975), Galton *et al.* (1980) and Bennett *et al.* (1984). All three considered gender, yet while the first two report virtually no social interaction between boys and girls, the third reports such interaction occurring freely and frequently. The differences could reflect the age of pupils, for Boydell and Galton *et al.* used older primary school pupils while Bennett *et al.* focused on six- to seven-year olds. However, they may also reflect a somewhat higher degree of structure to the contexts Bennett *et al.* observed, such that opting out of interaction was considerably more difficult. This may in turn stem from the early (and partial) application of the research discussed in the previous section: the Bennett *et al.* study was after all the most recent of the three pieces of work.

Whatever the reasons, it is unlikely, given the contradictions, that much will be gained by a lengthy review, and for this reason the remainder of the chapter will consider the experimental studies whose practical relevance remains to be seen. As with the previous chapter, the studies will be considered in terms first of methodology, then of results and finally of significance.

Experimental methodology in desk-based group work

Focusing then on the experimental studies, two points immediately become apparent. The first is that relatively few of the studies have paid attention to gender. The second is that virtually all of the ones that have considered gender have approached group organisation via the use of symmetric role structures, full collaboration in co-operative set ups, highly structured tasks, and incentive-free goals. Up to a point, the approach to group organisation is laudable, for it emulates what the research summarised earlier in the chapter suggests is 'best practice'. Nevertheless, it should be remembered that asymmetric role structures, that is structures where one pupil helps another rather than shares responsibility, may be preferable when the material involves the use of skills, and some of the studies used tasks which have a strong skills element. For this reason, we cannot be entirely certain that the studies are simulating the classroom practice of the future.

Looked at in greater detail, the studies turn out, like the research discussed in the previous chapter, to be multi-national, with the United States and Australasia represented as well as Britain. They cover a reasonably wide age range but with one striking gap: almost without exception, the pupils are aged ten or over. The omission of younger pupils is as surprising as it is disappointing for, as will become apparent in the final chapter, there is related research with nursery school samples. Thus, by omitting the five- to ten-year age group, opportunities to make direct links with the preschool experience seem to have been missed. On top of this, there are, unfortunately, further gaps once we turn to subject matter and grouping practices. In relation to the curriculum, mathematics and science swamp the field. In terms of grouping, the favoured approach has been to work with foursomes, ignoring all the other potential group sizes. This said, contrasts are made between mixed groups and same-sex, between balanced groups (that is two boys and two girls) and one sex in the majority, and between same-sex, balanced and majority groups. Thus a wide range of gender compositions are considered within the possibilities allowed by foursomes. Also, as befits their experimental status, the studies typically have designs which involve individual pretests, group-based interventions and individual post-tests, and thus, unlike the whole-class research, these studies provide information about both social interaction and learning outcome.

Gender differences in desk-based interaction

In terms of social interaction, the emphasis as regards dialogue has been on the requesting and giving of help, that is, 'I'm stuck, how do you do it?' and, 'You add the first number to the second number, and that's the answer.' A review of the literature conducted by Webb, N (1989) has shown that these variables can be crucial to the learning outcome, and so including them is certainly warranted. However, other variables are also important. American research (see, for example, Kruger, 1993) testifies to the importance of 'transactive' contributions, that is contributions which extend their immediate antecedent by challenging, justifying, or clarifying (for example 'I don't think that's a good idea because the sun will make the fish too hot' in reply to 'Let's put the tank by the window'). Moreover, recent fine-grained approaches to the study of dialogue have demonstrated the significance of dialogue which integrates discussion around a topic with other activities. Howe *et al.* (1995) have, for instance, shown that group work will facilitate pupils' understanding of physical mechanisms if, and only if, those mechanisms are used to resolve disagreements over the interpretation of outcomes and then 'referred back to' when subsequent predictions are being formulated. Further work by the same researchers has confirmed the importance of referring back in other contexts, suggesting that group support for the consolidation and comparison of earlier activity is a major influence on learning outcome.

It is a pity that none of these findings is reflected in the gender-based analyses, for it means that the picture from the latter is inevitably incomplete. However, taking the incompleteness for granted and focusing as a consequence on helping, Webb (1984) has shown that with groups of four organised for secondary-level mathematics, girls ask for help to a greater extent than boys. Furthermore, girls typically ask for general strategic explanations ('What kind of sum is it?'), while boys focus on specific procedural information ('Which column do you add first?') within already determined strategies. Analysed more closely though, the results arise because of marked differences in those groups where girls are in the majority. There are no differences in balanced groups or in groups where boys predominate. It is tempting to bring another of Webb's findings to bear here, that both girls and boys tend to address their requests to boys. After all, when girls are in a majority in groups of four, there will only be one boy within each group and the boys will not have another boy to address. If boys are seen by boys as the only acceptable sources of help, it is little wonder that they seek help less frequently than girls. This said, the interpretation could only apply to the quantitative differences in seeking help; it could not be relevant to the strategic versus procedural difference mentioned above.

On the giving of help, Webb's main findings are that girls' requests are twice as likely as boys' to be ignored, the upshot being that boys receive more explanations in total. The root of this is almost certainly the tendency, documented above, for both girls and boys to address their requests to boys, for boys are seemingly much more likely to respond to other boys than they are to girls. Interestingly, in the context of science both Webb and Conwell, Griffin & Algozzine (1993) find that girls are more likely to respond to requests than boys no matter what the requester's sex. The implication is that if girls were addressed more frequently, both sexes would receive more help and the boy-girl discrepancy might disappear. The findings related to responsiveness to requests seem to apply regardless of whether the groups are balanced or one sex is in the majority. However, Petersen, Johnson & Johnson (1991) claim a tendency towards equalisation of help-giving itself within balanced groups when compared with majority, and McCaslin, Tuck, Waird, Brown, Lapage & Pyle (1994) have evidence that balanced groups may be superior here relative to same-sex. Although the pupils whom McCaslin *et al.* observed in balanced groups were slower to engage in helping, they sustained their helping activities longer, such that over the full two weeks of the study they helped to a greater degree.

A picture is emerging, then, of balanced groups achieving the most supportive environment, and this may be surprising. However, a number of caveats need to be noted. Firstly, as already stressed, there is more to group dialogue than the requesting and giving of help, and the implications of gender for the other parameters are presently uncharted. Secondly, there is more to group interaction than dialogue, and studies which have looked beyond dialogue paint a picture which is considerably less rosy. For example, both Conwell *et al.* (1993) and Whyte (1984) find that boys monopolise the science apparatus in small-group practicals, and there is no suggestion of this becoming less severe in balanced groups. Whyte describes a situation so extreme that the boys ended up with all the safety goggles, and it was only after the teacher intervened that the girls were adequately protected. Rennie & Parker (1987) found that girls in same-sex pairs had more opportunities than girls in mixed pairs to manipulate equipment (mixed pairs necessarily being balanced in the sense of this chapter). Rennie & Parker comment that the girls in mixed pairs spent more time listening and watching than they did in same-sex, and less time actively involved. The boys were unaffected by group composition.

Desk-based group work and academic achievement

Do any of the gender differences charted above make substantive differences to academic achievement? As mentioned already, most of the studies had a pretest – intervention – posttest design, and thus by looking at before and after changes could explore the learning outcome. Unfortunately, the results are contradictory. In her mathematics study, Webb (1984) found that the boys obtained higher posttest scores than the girls despite being equal at pre-test, and Petersen *et al.* (1991) found the same on one of their two tests of scientific knowledge. However, McCaslin *et al.* (1994) found no gender differences on maths tests, while Smith *et al.* (1995) found girls making more progress. Smith *et al.* compared classes who experienced repeated cycles of whole-class instruction followed by group-based problem-solving (the 'experimental' classes) with classes whose whole-class instruction was followed by individual problem solving (the 'control' classes). The pupils in the experimental classes made more progress than the pupils in the control. However, within the experimental classes, the girls progressed about twice as much as the boys.

Seeking to reconcile the differences between the studies, the following can be excluded as relevant factors: (a) age differences, since all the studies apart from Webb's were with ten- to twelve-year olds; (b) ability differences, since all the studies controlled for ability; (c) subject matter differences, since all the studies except Petersen *et al.*'s were concerned with maths; and (d) type of knowledge differences, since Webb and McCaslin *et al.*'s studies were skills-based while Petersen *et al.* and Smith *et al.*'s were conceptual. Although only two of the studies (Webb and Smith *et al.*) provide the necessary data, a more likely factor is different kinds of relationships between help provision and learning outcome. Webb found that giving help was positively related to progress, and receiving help was negatively related or unrelated depending upon the form of help provided. Smith *et al.* found precisely the reverse, in other words that help giving was negatively related to progress and help receiving was positively related. We have already seen that boys are defined by both boys and girls as the givers of help and girls are correspondingly defined as the receivers. Thus the differences in how help provision relates to outcome could explain why Webb found boys gained most and Smith *et al.*, on the other hand, found that girls were the main beneficiaries.

Of course, the question is raised of why the two studies differed in the relationship they found between help provision and learning, and this has to be an issue for further research. Nevertheless, despite the fact that the interpretation of the differences is currently unchartable, it has to be worrying that access to the aspects of dialogue which appear central to learning, that is the giving and receiving of help, are bound up with gender. In terms of equivalent learning opportunities, it would be preferable for boys and girls to have equal access to the behaviours that matter. Indeed, without equal access, it is possible that when ordinary classrooms start deploying structured group work along the lines described in this section (and the assumption has been that eventually they will do this), the gender balance in academic achievement described by Powney (1996) and detailed in the previous chapter might be seriously disrupted.

This is not, of course, an argument against desk-based group work of a structured variety. On the contrary, virtually all of the studies discussed here attest to considerable academic benefits, often documenting 'added value' in comparison with traditional methods of teaching. Rather, the argument is for great care in how desk-based group work is organised in the schools of the future, assuming its implementation.

Noting this as a point for further development, the following list summarises what has already emerged:

- In structured group work girls ask for help to a greater extent than boys, particularly general strategic help.

- Both girls and boys prefer to ask boys for help. Since boys answer boys more often than girls, this can lead to girls' requests being ignored.

- Girls are more likely than boys to answer whatever requests for help are addressed to them.

- Groups where the sex distribution is balanced produce fewer asymmetries of dialogue than groups where either sex is in the majority.

- Boys monopolise apparatus regardless of group composition.

- As regards structured group work, there are no consistent associations between sex and learning outcome. However, it is likely that gender-differentiated aspects of interaction are relevant to outcome. This requires further research as a matter of urgency, so that schools can be guided as to how best to organise group work.

4

Group Work Around Computers

"There is very little evidence that gender differences in interaction around computers have a direct bearing on learning. If it has long-term academic consequences, it is more likely to be by inculcating relatively negative attitudes in girls which may result in their opting out of subjects and careers where computers are centrally involved."

The previous chapter made a strong distinction between group work as it currently operates in classrooms and group work as it may come to exist in the future, and one basis for the distinction was differences in the structuring of tasks. When pupils are seated in groups around their desks and given opportunities to collaborate, the tasks that they are currently provided with often lack structure. This should change if the evidence from experimental research is followed. However, while lack of structure is true of desk-based group tasks, it is not true of all current educational tasks. One exception is the use of educational software for this frequently has a high level of structure. This is an important area because although educational software is usually designed for individual usage, it is typically approached by pupils working in groups. Thus, through software, we have currently-used group tasks which do have structure in current use, and therefore group work around computers warrants separate treatment.

Documentary evidence of the group-based nature of computer use appears in two surveys, one by Jackson, Fletcher & Messer (1986) involving 110 Hertfordshire primary schools, and the other by McAteer & Demissie (1991) involving 111 Glasgow primary schools. Both surveys asked about individual versus group use for a range of types of software, for example problem-solving and data-handling, and both found that for the majority of types over 80% (and up to 97%) of usage was in groups. The only exceptions were drill-and-practice, which was in both surveys more or less evenly divided between individual and group usage, and word-processing which was not considered by Jackson *et al.* but which was also evenly divided in the McAteer & Demissie study. Accepting the group-based context of school computing, Crook (1987) and Light, Foot, Colbourn & McClelland (1987) have pointed out that this is often nothing more than a reflection of expediency. Computers are scarce resources in classrooms and so pupils share because there are not enough for individual use.

In their surveys, Jackson *et al.* and McAteer & Demissie also asked about the size and sex composition of groups. In terms of group size, Jackson *et al.* report 59% pairs or threesomes, 26% foursomes, and 15% five or more. Recast for comparability with Jackson *et al.*, the equivalent figures in McAteer & Demissie's study are 78%, 18% and 3%. Thus small groups predominate, with the distribution being slightly more skewed in the Scottish sample than in the English. As for sex, mixed groups predominated in both surveys to the tune of around 80%. Thinking about the implications of this for research into gender, studies might be expected which compare mixed groups with same-sex ones in the context of small groups and larger ones. Unfortunately, such studies are rare: only two attempts to vary both gender composition and group size have been unearthed, both American, and one of them (Guntermann & Tovar, 1987) was restricted to pairs and threesomes. So we are left with just one piece of research which considers gender while contrasting small with larger groups, a study by Berge (1990) which involved pairs and foursomes. As it happens, this failure to consider group size is symptomatic of the computer-based literature as a whole for, as is clear from a recent review by Stephenson (1994), the focus has been on groups versus individuals, and not on groups of varying sizes. The upshot has been that investigations of features such as gender have generally proceeded with the group size held constant. This has created real gaps in the literature, although it is noteworthy that neither Guntermann & Tovar nor Berge found group size to have a bearing on the gender effects revealed.

Methodological overview

Focusing then on research in computer contexts which considers gender without varying the size of the group, there is already a substantial body of material, virtually all dating from the mid-1980s. In the vast majority of cases, its chosen group size is pairs, although there are reports of groups as large as six (for example, Pozzi, Healy & Hoyles, 1993). Within the pair framework, most studies have contrasted boy/boy, boy/girl, and girl/girl arrangements. When the groups have been larger, there have usually been attempts to continue the same-sex, majority and balanced contrasts that featured so strongly in the desk-based studies of group work discussed in the last chapter. In terms of other features, British research into computer-based work is more prominent than in the material discussed earlier, with American and Australasian studies very much in the minority. All age groups from five to 15 have been covered, although the emphasis has been on seven- to twelve-year olds. LOGO is by far the most popular software featured, but there is work involving problem solving in science, literacy puzzles (both reading and writing), complex route planning, and geography.

In terms of research focus, a sizeable proportion of the studies have considered group interaction, both verbal and physical, using the combination of direct observation and tape-recording that featured in whole-class research. As with the whole-class research, the studies which use tape-recording (and this usually means video) have tended to be the more recent, although it is interesting that the shift from observation to recording took place several years later with the computer-based studies than it did with the whole-class. Somewhat fewer of the studies have looked at academic outcome, although there are still well over a dozen relevant studies. These studies use computer records or individual posttests (and sometimes both) to make assessments of outcome. What is seriously lacking, however, is research which relates interaction to the learning outcome. Nevertheless, despite this, this chapter can draw two reasonably definite conclusions:

■ Despite their apparent popularity with teachers, mixed groups are associated with reduced talk, social withdrawal, resentment and male dominance.

■ This may be relevant to the negative attitudes to computers which many girls develop and to the disproportionately high numbers of girls opting out of computer studies as a school subject.

Gender differences in interaction around computers

Starting with the research results relating to group interaction, work by Lee (1993) and by Tolmie & Howe (1993) indicates that, around computers, conversations are more extended in same-sex groups than in mixed. Tolmie & Howe found, for instance, that same-sex groups, both boy/boy and girl/girl, engaged in one-and-a-half times the number of switches of speaker than mixed groups did. However, while these results are suggestive, it should be noted that both Lee and Tolmie & Howe focused on the early secondary school age group, and that the latter found a steady decrease in such turntaking between twelve and 15. It may be that the pressures to avoid conversation between the sexes in computer environments are particularly acute in adolescence, a possibility rendered plausible by the failure of any of the studies with younger pupils to refer to differences in turntaking. Where the studies with young pupils make most contact with the studies with older pupils is over the form of turntaking when it occurs, for this has been a powerful theme throughout the research.

Unsurprisingly, attention has been paid once more to the giving and requesting of help. Two studies have shown that in mixed groups girls are more inclined to seek help from boys than the reverse, these being the Lee study cited above and an investigation by Siann & McLeod (1986) which involved five- to seven-year olds. According to Lee, girls also receive more help than boys in mixed groups, suggesting that their requests are being answered. This 'compliance' on the part of boys means that they are more likely to provide help in mixed environments than they are in same-sex. This said, the compliance is not always welcome: Siann & McLeod found that girls resent help from boys when they receive it practically rather than verbally. In other words, they dislike it intensely when boys manipulate the mouse or the keyboard on their behalf. From Lee's data, it appears that girls are most likely to provide help when they are in same-sex groups, an observation consistent with Underwood, Underwood & Turner's (1993) finding that girl/girl pairs suggest answers more frequently than do boy/boy pairs. Unfortunately, the help that girls receive in single-sex groups may not always be useful, for if we turn once more to Lee there is evidence that all-girl groups are the least likely of all gender combinations to come up with adequate answers to questions. There is, of course, a strong implication in this that the help which girls receive from other girls is inferior to the help that they receive from boys. As noted in the previous chapter, there is more to group interaction than helping. Thus, it is fortunate that, unlike the research discussed there, a number of additional perspectives exist with regard to computer-based interaction. The results are, however, very much of a piece with what has emerged from helping. For example, work by Fitzpatrick & Hardman (1994) and Underwood, McCaffrey & Underwood (1990) indicates that boy/girl pairs are less inclined to negotiate, in other words to engage in what were earlier called transactions. Compared with both boy/boy pairs and girl/girl, claims in boy-girl pairs are asserted rather than discussed. Likewise, there is evidence that the boys in mixed groups dominate interactions physically. Barbieri & Light (1992), Fitzpatrick & Hardman (1994), Siann, McLeod, Glissov & Durndell (1990) and Underwood *et al.* (1993) have all observed extreme asymmetries of control of the keyboard and mouse in mixed groups, with the boys always dominant. Barbieri & Light and Underwood *et al.* also find differences between all-boy and all-girl groups, with the latter showing the greatest balance of roles. One exception to the dominance patterns should however be noted, the work of Bergin, Ford & Hess (1993). This work is interesting because it was conducted with very young children, aged five to six in fact, suggesting that the gender differences may emerge during schooling.

Faced though with the normal pattern of male dominance in mixed groups, it is hard to resist tying it with the evidence already documented that girls feel resentment when they receive physical help. Nevertheless, while this association may be justified, it does not look as if the resentment is displayed overtly during the interaction. In the first place, Guntermann & Tovar (1987) found that girls express more agreement than boys in both mixed and same-sex groups, and their levels of agreement in the two kinds of group are roughly equivalent. Since overt resentment should reduce the frequency of agreement, these results can be taken as indirect evidence for lack of overt resentment within mixed groups. In addition, mixed groups are not associated with high levels of antagonism. On the contrary, Guntermann & Tovar, Lee (1993) and

Underwood *et al.* (1993) found that when antagonism was displayed in computer-based groupings, it was most pronounced in groups consisting of boys. Against this it is true that, in their work with groups of six, Pozzi *et al.* (1993) observed that when groups broke down this was typically along sex lines. However, they report that this could mean one boy versus three girls versus two boys, implying that antagonism between boys could still have been responsible. In fact, Tolmie & Howe (1993) suggest that the reaction of mixed pairs to points of possible conflict is withdrawal rather than confrontation, leading, of course, to the reduced turntaking that has already been documented. Working with physics software, Tolmie & Howe presented a series of problems where groups were pressed to articulate views and resolve disagreements: with the same-sex pairs, the more they disagreed the more they discussed; with the mixed sex, the more they disagreed, the more they inclined to silence.

Implications of computer-based group work

From the previous section, it is easy to form a very negative impression of interactions in mixed-sex groups in computer environments, and up to a point that would be warranted. However, it is important not to lose sight of the point made earlier, namely that the help girls receive from boys seems to be superior to the help they receive from other girls. Thus, hypothesising about the implications for learning is far from straightforward. There may be no relation between interaction and learning, but if there is it could take at least three forms. Firstly, it is possible that, thanks to their interaction patterns, pupils dislike mixed groups relative to same-sex groups, but, because of the quality of help giving, mixed groups are still better for learning than all-girl groups. Secondly, it is possible that mixed groups are disliked relative to same-sex groups, and for that reason they are also detrimental to learning. Finally, it is possible that mixed-sex groups are academically better for girls than same-sex groups, and for that reason they are liked better, despite their apparently poor social environment. In reality, the final possibility can be rejected straightforwardly: Barbieri & Light (1992) found that the girls in boy/girl pairs were less happy with their partners than the girls in girl/girl pairs, the boys in boy/boy pairs, and the boys in boy/girl pairs.

The academic consequences are less easily dealt with, for the research proves contradictory. Consistent with the first of the three possibilities cited above (ie not popular but better academically), Hughes, Brackenridge, Bibby & Greenhough (1989) found mixed groups performing better on a LOGO task than all-girl, and the same as all-boy. However, Hughes & Greenhough (1991) report failure to replicate this in four follow-up studies which used equivalent procedures. Consistent with the second possibility (mixed groups bad academically because unpopular), Dalton (1990) and Underwood *et al.* (1990) found all-boy and all-girl groups performing equivalently to each other and better than mixed. Underwood, Jindal & Underwood (1994) found the same so long as the groups adopted a cooperative style of interaction. However, consistent with neither possibility are the findings of Barbieri & Light (1992) that boys are more successful than girls regardless of pairing; of Littleton, Light, Joiner, Messer & Barnes (1992), Underwood *et al.* (1990), Yelland (1994) and Fitzpatrick & Hardman (1994) that boys' performance improves more rapidly than girls but there are no differences eventually; and of Guntermann & Tovar (1987), Pozzi *et al.* (1993), Underwood *et al.* (1993), Issroff (1994) and Tolmie & Howe (1993) that there is no association whatsoever between gender and performance.

Some sense is beginning to be made of these results. Littleton *et al.* (1992), for instance, have shown that the software content makes more difference to girls than it does to boys. Thus, while girls performed worse than boys on a 'masculine' adventure game (involving, for example, pirates), their performance was similar to boys when the same task was presented with 'gender-neutral' content. However, by calling on content, Littleton *et al.* are shifting the focus from group interaction, implying a belief that the latter is not a major determinant of learning outcome. On the face of it, they would seem likely to be right: given that the bulk of the studies obtained results which are not compatible with any model which centralises interaction, it is hard to find grounds for using interaction to explain differences in outcome. However, this does not mean that interaction is irrelevant to learning, for it may affect the learning *process* even if it has no bearing on outcome. Strong evidence that it does appears in Tolmie & Howe (1993), one of the few studies to attempt a direct analysis of the relationship between interaction and outcome. As noted above, Tolmie & Howe found no differences in the learning gains made after participation in boy/boy, boy/girl and girl/girl pairs. However, they did find marked differences in the features of dialogue that were relevant to learning across the three types of pairs, suggesting differences in how the material was being appropriated. Boy/boy pairs tended to focus their discussions on the feedback which the computer provided, that is whether their solutions to problems were right or wrong. Girl/girl pairs, by contrast, were more interested in the structure of the problem being solved, and how it related to problems encountered earlier. Beyond this, Tolmie & Howe also found that dialogue was less important for learning in the boy/girl pairs than in the same sex, indicating that the former were compensating for their discomfort by learning from the software and not from each other.

The implication is, then, that the non-congenial social environment does not jeopardise learning, a conclusion which relates closely to points raised in relation to whole-class interaction. However, a lack of effect on learning does not necessarily mean that group work with computers has no long-term consequences. The line taken in the first chapter was that pupils can be turned off school subjects not simply by experiences of failure but also by feeling marginalised. Even if we decide that interaction around computers has limited relevance via the first route, we may feel that it is significant via the second. Certainly, the survey evidence summarised by Powney (1996) shows that computing studies is one of the few subjects where girls opt out relative to boys, with only about one-third of recent Scottish Standard Grade candidates being female. Thus, there is a gender imbalance in computing, and group interaction may have something to do with it. After all, as we saw at the start of this chapter, Jackson *et al.* (1986) and McAteer (1991) found that mixed groups are the most common pattern in classrooms, and the evidence presented here has shown mixed groups to be particularly discomforting for girls. In addition, Siann *et al.* (1990) show that girls have relatively negative attitudes to computers when compared with boys, and these are intensified by classroom experiences.

Gender differences in pupils' interaction around computers could therefore be extremely significant, and they will be returned to in the final chapter. However, to sum up for now:

■ Single-sex groups talk more in computer environments than mixed groups, at least at the secondary school level.

■ Girls are more likely to request help from boys than the reverse.

■ The help that boys give can be resented especially if it is physical.

■ Boys dominate computers physically at all but the youngest age levels.

■ There is more antagonism in all-male groups, more agreement in all female groups, and mixed groups are characterised by a lack of social contact.

■ Girls who work in mixed groups enjoy the computing experience less than boys in mixed and single-sex groups and girls in single-sex groups. Since mixed groups are the most common in schools, this may be worrying.

■ There is very little evidence that gender differences in interaction around computers has a direct bearing on learning. If it has long-term academic consequences, it is more likely to be by inculcating relatively negative attitudes in girls which may result in their opting out of subjects and careers where computers are centrally involved.

5

Oral Assessment

"Preliminary indications are that discussion sessions for oral assessment are either stilted or gender-differentiated. When gender differences occur, they may have implications for the grades assigned."

The research considered so far relates to gender effects in the learning situation. However social interaction has also, relatively recently, entered the assessment process, through the introduction of 'oral assessment' into the GCSE in England, Wales and Northern Ireland and the Standard Grade in Scotland. In the light of this, it is desirable to look at this area, to see, firstly, if there are gender differences in the form that assessment interactions take and, secondly, if those differences are reflected in the grades obtained. This can only be done to the extent that there is relevant work, and because the development is fairly new, there is very little, in fact, only two studies, the work of Cheshire and Jenkins in England (see Jenkins & Cheshire, 1990; Cheshire & Jenkins, 1991) and of Wareing (1994) in Scotland. Obviously, two investigations are not sufficient to draw conclusions, particularly as the results are not entirely consistent with each other. Nevertheless, given both the importance of the matter in its own right and the contrast with the material discussed so far, the studies are reviewed here, if only to set the scene for further research. The major conclusions include:

- ■ Preliminary indications are that discussion sessions for oral assessment are either stilted or gender-differentiated.
- ■ When gender differences occur, they may have implications for the grades assigned.

Gender differences in assessed discussions

The background to the two investigations is somewhat different from the material discussed earlier, the approach being socio-linguistic rather than educational or psychological. Socio-linguistic approaches to social interaction are concerned with form and function relations, that is relationships between meanings and the words, phrases and so on which are used to express them. Educational and psychological approaches are usually restricted to functions. The key consequence for present purposes is the use of categories which are both different from and more specific than those encountered previously. There are, nevertheless, obvious parallels, with 'back-channel comments' ('uh-hu' or 'yeah') instead of 'expressing agreement' and 'interruption' instead of 'dominance'.

Bearing the differences in mind, the seminal sociolinguistic work relating to gender (and the work which stimulated the investigations of oral assessment) is that associated with Lakoff (1974, 1975). Based on casual observations of herself and her associates, Lakoff listed a number of stylistic features that she believed to characterise women's speech. Although not organised in this way by Lakoff, the features can be placed into two main classes. The first class amounts to features which render women's speech 'nicer' than men's, such as the supposedly greater tendency of women to aim for received grammars and accents, to use politeness markers such as 'please' and 'thank you', and to use weaker expletives. The second class includes features which render women's speech more tentative than men's, for example the supposedly greater tendency of women to use question intonation where intonation for a statement might be expected, to insert hedges like 'well', 'y'know', 'I mean' where they might be omitted, and to conclude with tags like 'isn't it', 'aren't they' where they add nothing to the content.

As Lakoff's proposals were becoming known (and indeed while her reports were still circulating in manuscript and not actually published), other features were added within the same framework. For example, it is certainly not 'nice' to interrupt speakers before they have finished speaking, and Zimmerman & West (1975) found evidence that interruptions are more frequent in conversations between the sexes than they are in single-sex. Furthermore, when they occur, they are almost always men interrupting women. Similarly, it is 'nice' to show speakers that you are interested in what they have to say by using back-channel comments such as uh-hu, and Hirshmann (1973, 1974) claimed that back-channel comments are particularly characteristic of women.

Over the past 20 years, there have been numerous attempts to see whether the stylistic features do vary with gender as proposed (for summaries of the results, see Coates, 1986; Coates & Cameron, 1989; Wardhaugh, 1992). Some of the features are more robust than others. For example, compared with men, women do appear to make greater use of received forms, questions, hedges, and back-channel comments, and they do appear predominant amongst the victims of interruption but there is very little evidence to support the claims about tags. Furthermore, politeness and expletives remain mysterious. One point that emerges clearly from the research is that the strength of the gender differences varies with the context. However, there is nothing to suggest that oral assessment would be immune and it was to establish what happens to the stylistic features within that context that the work of Cheshire & Jenkins and Wareing proceeded.

Both studies were relatively small-scale: the Cheshire and Jenkins study (see Jenkins & Cheshire, 1990) involved three groups each containing three girls and two boys, and the Wareing study involved seven groups containing three to five pupils, with three groups being all girl, one being all-boy and three being mixed. In both studies, the groups held discussions which they knew would be marked as part of continuously assessed oral work. Cheshire and Jenkins found that, averaged across participants, the boys did indeed interrupt more than the girls, although this was largely due to the extreme intrusiveness of a single individual. The girls also ran true to form by producing more back-channel comments and more questions, the latter being used as conversational gambits to engage their partners. Wareing, by contrast, found none of these things, although she did find other signs of 'partner engagement' amongst the girls and also more echoing by girls of what had just been said, a behaviour which has been seen by some theorists as equivalent to back-channel. Wareing also found an inverse relation between amount of speaking and amount of back-channel, although neither of these features was gender-related.

Implications for grades

It is not immediately apparent why the two sets of results differ, although it could be that Wareing's discussions were relatively inhibited. She reported that the overall level of interruptions was low, and this can be taken as indicating rather stilted discussions (see Rutter, 1989). Indeed, it can also be related to the suggestion in Beattie's (1981) data that gender differences diminish as inhibitions increase. This said, if the argument is correct, teachers preparing pupils for oral assessment would seem to be left with a choice between stilted discussions or gender differences. Is this the proverbial devil and the deep blue sea? Certainly, stilted discussions are undesirable: in a later study involving 23 teachers grading video-recorded discussions, Wareing found that, overall, talkativeness was a powerful predictor of grades. However, what about gender differences?

Lakoff's (1974, 1975) view on the significance of gender differences for any kind of judgment would have been that they should not matter, for she saw women as 'damned if they do and damned if they don't'. They are damned if they do (meaning do use the female speech style) because they are open to perceptions of frivolity, and damned if they do not because (unlike men who are regarded as assertive) they are seen as boorish. A similar sense of double standard appears in Spender's (1982) work, where she argues that women are seen as chatty despite talking less than men because silence is the cultural expectation regarding women. Experimental research has not, however, borne either of them out. There have been numerous studies looking at evaluations of communicative style and evaluations of communicators, when both the female style and its male counterpart are used by men and women. Examples include Erickson, Lind, Johnson & O'Barr's (1978) investigation of courtroom testimony, and Locksley, Ortiz & Hepburn's (1980) study of written texts. They both found that positive evaluations were dependent on use of the male speech style regardless of sex of speaker.

Thus, speech style appears to matter, and the female style comes off worst. Women are damned if they do, but then so are men and neither are damned if they don't. Where does this leave us as regards oral assessment, given that the evidence of Cheshire and Jenkins at least suggests that even in this context the gender differences occur? In the second of their two papers Cheshire and Jenkins (1991) attempted to find out by playing tape recordings of their three discussion groups to four teachers, and asking the teachers to make assessments and explain what their assessments were based on. Several points emerge. First, the teachers recognised the significance of back-channel remarks in facilitating dialogue. However, they found it difficult to register its frequency, and so give credit to it in assigning grades. Second, the lack of content in questions was used to mark pupils down, regardless of the fact that these also had a function in sustaining conversation. Third, interruptions were not regarded favourably, and the boy who interrupted frequently was correspondingly marked down. However, interruptions were seldom distinguished from other forms of simultaneous speech, including the empathic repetition which Wareing reported as being characteristic of girls.

Taking all the points together, Cheshire and Jenkins argue that the facilitating skills that girls displayed were not always rewarded as they deserved, and were indeed sometimes tarred by association with male interruption. Obviously, the argument has to be treated as suggestive rather than definitive when it is based on 15 pupils only. Nevertheless, it is revealing that APU surveys in England, Wales and Ireland throughout the 1980s have found no gender differences in the grades awarded on spoken language tests, while girls do consistently better on reading and writing tests (see Swann (1992) for details).

To sum up:

- ▪ Preliminary investigations of discussions for oral assessment suggest that they are either inhibited or gender-differentiated.
- ▪ When gender-differentiated, they are in line with the results of other socio-linguistic investigations, with boys interrupting more and girls showing a variety of behaviours which sustain conversations.
- ▪ Interruption is penalised in assigning grades, but conversation-sustaining behaviours may not be given their full credit.

6

Conclusions

The preceding chapters have reviewed the research relating to classroom interaction in four distinct contexts. In each of these contexts, marked gender differences have been found. The time has now come to pull the differences together, and to gain an overall impression of what they mean. This will be the substance of this chapter, with discussion organised into three main parts. First, the major findings are extracted from the preceding chapters, and synthesised under some common themes. Then Delamont's (1990) claim is revisited, that classroom interaction makes an active contribution to the gender divisions which exist in society. Two questions are asked: whether the gender differences in classroom interaction are relevant to divisions in society and whether classroom interaction actively creates the differences. Finally, the implications for action are discussed, with action being interpreted in terms of further research and classroom intervention.

A synthesis of the findings

Probably the most striking point to emerge from the research is that contributions from boys predominate during classroom interaction. In whole-class sessions where the decisions about who contributes are usually made by teachers, boys make more contributions than girls, and their contributions are usually more elaborate. They achieve their higher levels of contribution partly through activities within the discussion sessions, for example hand-raising and restlessness, and partly through reputations for misbehaviour which lead to greater monitoring by teachers. In small group work where rights to contribute are resolved between pupils, boys usually have the upper hand. They dominate the physical context, volunteering for practical demonstrations in science and controlling the mouse and keyboard in computing. They do the same where the emphasis is on talk. Research into oral assessment suggests that boys interrupt girls more than the reverse. Although interruption has not been studied in other contexts, the assertive rather than negotiating style reported for mixed-sex work with computers suggests a similar pattern. In addition, boys ensure their dominance by establishing themselves as sources of help, for the research shows that boys are asked for help more than girls are.

There are signs in the research that girls are not always happy about the situation. An example is the resentment that they show when they receive physical help from boys during group work with computers. However, this dissatisfaction must not be over-stated, for there are further signs in the research that girls do not merely comply with the situation but in some respects help to create it. In structured group work, girls request help more often than boys, and when they are in mixed groups girls direct their requests to boys. In detail, the evidence suggests that with the two-member groups which are typical within computer environments, girls more likely to request help from boys than reverse. In larger groups where both sexes are available as potential sources of help, both boys and girls address requests for help to boys. Indeed, a greater tendency on the part of girls to request help from others is a second major theme throughout the research, for parallel evidence was presented for whole-class contexts. There it was found that girls approach teachers for individual help more than boys do.

Although girls are relatively likely to seek help, they are not unwilling to give help when asked. On the contrary, the research suggests that in structured group work girls are more likely than boys to respond to the requests addressed to them. It is simply that fewer requests for help are addressed to girls in the first place. Indeed, it would be somewhat surprising if girls were not relatively willing to offer help. Looked at more broadly, offering help is one instance of being conversationally supportive, and there is evidence throughout the research of girls supporting their conversational partners to a greater extent than boys do. A clear illustration of this appeared in the work on oral assessment, where, compared with boys, girls were found to produce more back-channel remarks, more empathic repetitions, and more questions which initiated conversation. In addition, there was the evidence in the computer-based work of girls expressing more agreement. Indeed, insofar as the agreements are directed to boys, a further general point can be made, that boys have more experience than girls of having their contributions evaluated during classroom interaction. After all, the whole-class research also showed that boys receive more positive and negative feedback on the contributions which they make.

Summing the findings up, then, four key points have emerged and these can be usefully repeated:

■ Contributions from boys predominate both physically and verbally during classroom interaction.

■ Girls request help to a greater extent than boys do.

■ Girls support their conversational partners to a greater extent than boys do.

■ Boys have more experience than girls of having their contributions evaluated during classroom interaction.

Social interaction and gender divisions

Synthesising the findings still further, it might be fair to say that boys typically are more focal than girls during classroom interaction. The substantive contributions, relating to the subject being taught, come from them, and it is these contributions which become the focus of feedback. If girls have roles, these are usually less obvious, involving eliciting contributions from others and supporting contributions when they occur. During whole-class sessions teachers fulfil the elicitation and feedback function, and so, in that context, girls are effectively silenced. These differences can partially be interpreted in terms of male dominance and female submissiveness, or male activity and female passivity. Evidence has, after all, been presented that boys push themselves forward in speech and physical action. While acknowledging this, there is more to the differences than can be placed on dominance/submissiveness or activity/passivity dimensions. Girls typically defer to boys in the competition for turns but their roles in conversations cannot be fully characterised in terms of submission or passivity. Soliciting contributions is a highly active process, and girls do this more frequently than boys.

Differences have then to be recognised but what is their significance? Do they contribute to the gender divisions in society or are they passing events, of immediate concern perhaps but of no long-term consequence? The question has been touched on throughout but three points can be made to bring the conclusions together.

The first is that there is little reason to think that the gender differences in classroom interaction have a direct bearing on academic performance. It is true that some of the studies described in previous chapters showed gender differences in learning achieved after gender-differentiated classroom sessions. Nevertheless, the nature of the differences were not always consistent from study to study, and they could seldom be related directly to patterns of interaction. In addition, the expectation is surely that if classroom interaction bears directly on academic performance, girls ought to be suffering, as they are, after all, the ones who seemingly take the minor roles in conversations. However, as has been stressed repeatedly, recent surveys show few differences in the academic performance of boys and girls, and where differences exist they usually show girls to be doing better than boys.

The second point is that classroom interaction may affect pupils' attitudes. This emerged most clearly in relation to computer-based work, where the physical control by boys was resented by girls. Could this be general? If it is, it might also apply to the science laboratory where boys were found to control the physical arena by participating more in laboratory demonstrations and having greater access to apparatus. The avoidance of computer studies by girls has already been commented on but the same applies to the physical sciences (again see Powney, 1996). It is hard to resist proposing a connection, even though the evidence for a direct link is not currently available.

Is it then the physical side of classroom interaction that is important? Possibly yes, as regards subject choice. Nevertheless a further point made in earlier chapters should not be forgotten and this attaches an equivalent, if different, significance to verbal interaction. What has now been called the 'conversationally focal' position of boys gives them experience of being listened to and responded to within the public domain. The experience of girls is to do the listening and, to some extent, the responding. When girls' voices are heard, it is in a more private context. As has been argued throughout, the difference may be relevant to career paths, in particular to the achievement of status and influence within employment and, perhaps relatedly, to the relative weight attached to occupational and domestic priorities. Certainly Woods (1989) found many of the now-familiar gender differences recurring in workplace discussions. Men interrupted women at work more than women interrupted men, and women offered more conversational support to men than the reverse. Importantly, the design of Woods' research meant that the differences could be shown to relate strongly to gender and weakly, but still positively, to occupational status. This is exactly what would be expected if, as hypothesised, gender differences in conversational behaviour predate but bear upon gender differences in occupational standing.

Suppose we concede then that classroom interaction, both physical and verbal, does have long-term consequences for gender divisions. Should we claim, as Delamont (1990) did, that schools play an active role in bringing the divisions into existence? Might it not be that schools merely perpetuate tendencies which already exist? Certainly, it would be hard to conclude from this review that teachers are responsible for every gender difference which has been found to exist. The whole-class research, for instance, suggested that the selection by teachers of boys is to some extent managed by the boys themselves. In addition, however, there are indications that pre-school children display at least some of the relevant differences. Haas (1979) observed boys talking more than girls in mixed pairs by the age of four, and Cook, Fritz, McCornack & Visperas (1985) obtained similar results for same-sex pairs. Based on a content analysis of what the children said, Cook *et al.* further concluded that the boys were already showing signs of 'leadership' in the statements they made. Thompson (1994) observed two- to five-year olds working on a jigsaw puzzle in the presence of an adult. He found that the girls were three times as likely as the boys to ask the adult for help.

Probably, then, children are already armed with gender-differentiated patterns of social interaction when they come to school. However, this does not necessarily mean that everything is settled by the age of five. In the first place, schools are clearly providing opportunities for the patterns to be practised and consolidated. In addition, there is evidence that some gender differences emerge for the first time during schooling. Mention has already been made of the research by Bergin *et al.* (1993) in computer environments. The study was with five- to six-year olds, and it was the exception to the rule of male dominance at the keyboard. In fact, further points of interest emerge from the results, in particular that in this young age-group girls were just as interested in the computers as boys, and that neither sex showed signs of antagonism and competitiveness. Coupled with the evidence of Siann *et al.* (1990) that girls' dislike of computing grows (rather than declines) with familiarity, this suggests strongly that the school experience does more than simply tolerate what already exists.

School and classroom practice

Probably this is about as far as it is currently possible go on the question of whether the social interaction which occurs in classrooms actively promotes the gender divisions which exist in society. Classroom interaction may be relevant to gender divisions far beyond those which occur in schools. Moreover, although classroom interaction builds on pre-school tendencies, it is probably not entirely determined by these. Thus, to the extent that it is relevant to gender divisions, it could be said to be actively promoting them. Should anything be done?

As pointed out already, there are two possible responses. One is to focus on the current uncertainties within the research, and to suggest waiting until matters are clearer. Another is to say that there is sufficient circumstantial evidence to warrant action. Tilting the balance towards the latter seems to be one piece of evidence that cannot be denied: the discomfort that girls feel at being pushed out of the centre of the action. Girls find other ways of coping so that their schoolwork does not suffer but they do not appear to enjoy their classroom roles to the same extent as boys. Evidence has already been presented which is relevant to this but mention should also be made of a survey by Daly, Kreiser & Roghaar (1994) which asked pupils about their general school experience. This study involved over 24,000 pupils, and it found, quite straightforwardly, that boys felt more positively about classroom interaction than girls. The survey is American, but if the results can be taken to apply in Britain, they suggest rather strongly that something should be done. Of course taking action will not be easy. The emphasis of this book is on relatively subtle behaviours. For reasons outlined at the beginning, no attention has been paid to blatant sexism. The trouble is that because the behaviours are subtle, teachers may find it hard to address them. Whyte (1984) provides useful information here through her work on the Girls into Science and Technology project. As mentioned earlier, this project aimed to train teachers in interactive strategies which would improve girls' attitudes and participation in the context of science. Whyte reports that teachers were surprised at how much attention they normally gave to boys. Moreover when they tried to alter their behaviour to achieve equal attention, they felt that they were devoting disproportionately more time to girls. This made them feel uncomfortable, and several reported that they were being unfair to the boys.

However, while the difficulties of implementation must be recognised, they are no excuse for not making an effort, and perhaps, in contrast to Girls into Science and Technology, focusing on the primary age group as well as the secondary. As already pointed out, there is probably no age in the five to 17 range at which gender differences cannot be observed. Nevertheless, if the line taken in this book is correct, these differences will be less entrenched and therefore less resistant to change at the early stages. In addition, however, if an intervention programme is attempted, it should not simply be addressed to classroom interaction as it currently exists. The chapter on desk-based group work focused on classrooms of the future, involving highly structured group tasks and greater attention to division of roles. Although futuristic, the scenario is nevertheless likely to happen, and it has definite implications for gender which it is important to recognise in designing attempts to change things.

A research agenda

Obviously any intervention programme should be carefully evaluated, and this most definitely should be on the research agenda for the future. However, it is clear that there are other matters which need to be addressed. The research to date has been primarily descriptive, and when it has gone beyond description it has focused almost entirely on learning outcomes. There may be a case for further description: as noted already, very little of the evidence comes from Scotland; when the work comes from Britain, it tends to be relatively small-scale; and even the large-scale studies from Australasia and the United States have focused on mathematics and science. So, there are gaps which could usefully be filled. However, if descriptive work is attempted, the recommendation here is that it should be located in a project which attempts to put description within a wider context. Pupils should be asked how they reacted to lessons which are gender-differentiated in the manner described in this book. For instance, when pupils are observed making informal approaches to teachers, they should be asked why they are doing this and how they feel about it. To permit linkages with the wider social context, attitudes and social attributions would seem to have as much of a role to play as description. Recognising this, the message is for a social psychological approach to future research.

Thus, finally, to conclude:

- Gender differences undoubtedly exist in classroom interaction, and they have the effect of making boys more focal within the teaching process.
- Although girls do not suffer academically because of these differences, they do feel more negatively about the school experience.
- For this reason, quite apart from longer term implications for gender divisions in society, something may need to be done to address the matter.
- If intervention is attempted, it should be carefully evaluated.
- At the same time, further research is needed to document gender differences, and more importantly to understand their consequences for pupils' perceptions of their place in society.

References

Barbieri, M S & Light, P H (1992) Interaction, gender, and performance on a computer-based problem solving task. *Learning and Instruction*, 2, 199–213.

Barnes, D (1973) *Language in the Classroom*. Milton Keynes: Open University Press.

Beattie, G W (1981) Interruption in conversational interaction, and its relation to the sex and status of the interactants. *Linguistics*, 19, 15–35.

Bennett, S N, Desforges, C W, Cockburn, A & Wilkinson, B (1984) *The Quality of Pupil Learning Experiences*. Lawrence Erlbaum.

Berge, Z (1990) Effects of group size, gender, and ability grouping on learning science process skills using microcomputers. *Journal of Research in Science Teaching*, 27, 747–759.

Bergin, D, Ford, M & Hess, R (1993) Patterns of motivation and social behaviour associated with microcomputer use of young children. *Journal of Educational Psychology*, 85, 437–445.

Bousted, M W (1989) Who talks? The position of girls in mixed sex classrooms. *English in Education*, 23, 41–51.

Boydell, D (1975) Pupil behaviour in junior classrooms. *British Journal of Educational Psychology*, 45, 122–129.

Cheshire, J & Jenkins, J (1991) Gender issues in the GCSE English exam: Part II. *Language and Education*, 5, 19–40.

Coates, J (1986) *Women, Men and Language*. Longman.

Coates, J & Cameron, D (1989) *Women in their Speech Communities*. Longman.

Conwell, C, Griffin, S & Algozzine, B (1993) Gender and racial differences in unstructured learning groups in science. *International Journal of Science Education*, 15, 107–115.

Cook, A, Fritz, J, McCornack, B & Visperas, C (1985) Early gender differences in the functional usage of language. *Sex Roles*, 12, 909–915.

Crook, C (1987) Computers in the classroom: defining a social context. In: Crook, C & Rutkowska, J C (eds) *Computers, Cognition and Development*. Chichester: John Wiley.

Daly, J, Kreiser, P & Roghaar, L (1994) Question-asking comfort: explorations of the demography of communication in the eighth grade classroom. *Communication Education*, 43, 27–41.

Dalton, D W (1990) The effects of cooperative learning strategies on achievement and attitudes during interactive video. *Journal of Computer-Based Instruction*, 17, 8–16.

Damon, W & Phelps, E (1989) Critical distinctions among three approaches to peer education. *International Journal of Educational Research*, 5, 331–343.

Dart, B & Clarke, J (1988) Sexism in schools: a new look. *Educational Review*, 40, 41–49.

Delamont, S (1990) *Sex Roles and the School*. Methuen.

Edwards, D & Mercer, N (1987) *Common Knowledge: The Development of Understanding in the Classroom*. Methuen.

Erickson, B, Lind, A E, Johnson, B C & O'Barr, W M (1978) Speech style and impression formation in a court setting: the effects of 'powerful' and 'powerless' speech. *Journal of Experimental Social Psychology*, 14, 266–279.

Fitzpatrick, H & Hardman, M (1994) Gender and the classroom computer: do girls lose out? In: Foot, H C, Howe, C J, Anderson, A, Tolmie, A & Warden, D (eds) *Group and Interactive Learning*. Southampton: Computational Mechanics.

Flanders, N A (1970) *Analysing Teacher Behaviour*. Reading, Mass: Addison-Wesley.

French, J & French, P (1984) Gender imbalances in the classroom: an interactional account. *Educational Research*, 26, 127–136.

Galton, M, Simon, B & Croll, P (1980) *Inside the Primary School*. Routledge & Kegan Paul.

Gillies, R M & Ashman, A F (1994) The effects on students of structured co-operative learning. In: Foot, H C, Howe, C J, Anderson, A, Tolmie, A & Warden, D (eds) *Group and Interactive Learning*. Southampton: Computational Mechanics.

Good, T, Cooper, H & Blakely, S (1980) Classroom interaction as a function of teacher expectations, student sex and time of year. *Journal of Educational Psychology*, 72, 378–385.

Good, T, Sikes, N & Brophy, J (1973) Effects of teacher sex, student sex on classroom interaction. *Journal of Educational Psychology*, 65, 74–87.

Guntermann, E & Tovar, M (1987) Collaborative problem-solving with LOGO: effects of group size and group composition. *Journal of Educational Computing Research*, 3, 313–334.

Haas, A (1979) Male and female spoken language differences: stereotypes and evidence. *Psychological Bulletin*, 86, 616–626.

Hirschmann, L (1973) Female-male differences in conversational interaction. Paper presented to the Linguistic Society of America.

Hirschmann, L (1974) Analysis of supportive and assertive behaviour in conversations. Paper presented to the Linguistic Society of America.

Howe, C J, Rodgers, C & Tolmie, A (1990) Physics in the primary school: peer interaction and the understanding of floating and sinking. *European Journal of Psychology of Education*, V, 459–475.

Howe, C J, Tolmie, A, Greer, K & Mackenzie, M (1995) Peer collaboration and conceptual growth in physics: task influences on children's understanding of heating and cooling. *Cognition and Instruction*, 13, 483–503.

Howe, C J, Tolmie, A & Rodgers, C (1992) The acquisition of conceptual knowledge in science by primary school children: group interaction and the understanding of motion down an incline. *British Journal of Developmental Psychology*, 10, 113–130.

Hughes, M, Brackenridge, A, Bibby, A & Greenhough, P (1989) Girls, boys and turtles: gender effects in young children learning with LOGO. In: Hoyles, C (ed) *Girls and Computers*. Bedford Way Papers, 34.

Hughes, M & Greenhough, P (1991) Research report and discussion I. Paper presented at ESRC InTER Seminar on 'Groupwork with Computers', Aston University.

Issroff, K (1994) Gender and cognitive and affective aspects of cooperative learning. In: Foot, H C, Howe, C J, Anderson, A, Tolmie, A & Warden, D (eds) *Group and Interactive Learning*. Southampton: Computational Mechanics.

Jackson, A, Fletcher, B C & Messer, D J (1986) A survey of microcomputer use and provision in primary schools. *Journal of Computer Assisted Learning*, 2, 45–44.

Jenkins, N & Cheshire, J (1990) Gender issues in the GCSE oral English examination: Part I. *Language and Education*, 4, 261–292.

Johnson, D W & Johnson, R T (1995) Positive interdependence: key to effective co-operation. In: Hertz-Lazarowitz, R & Miller, N (eds) *Interaction in Co-operative Groups: The Theoretical Anatomy of Group Learning*. Cambridge University Press.

Jones, M & Gerig, T (1994) Silent sixth-grade students: characteristics, achievement, and teacher expectations. *The Elementary School Journal*, 95, 169–182.

Jones, G & Wheatley, J (1989) Gender influences in classroom displays and student-teacher behaviour. *Science Education*, 73, 535–545.

Kruger, A C (1993) Peer collaboration: conflict, co-operation or both? *Social Development*, 2, 165–182.

Lakoff, R (1974) Why women are ladies. *Berkeley Studies in Syntax and Semantics*, 1, XV.

Lakoff, R (1975) *Language and Woman's Place*. New York: Harper Row.

Lee, M (1993) Gender, group composition, and peer interaction in computer-based cooperative learning. *Journal of Educational Computing Research*, 9, 549–577.

Light, P, Foot, T, Colbourn, C & McClelland, I (1987) Collaborative interactions at the microcomputer keyboard. *Educational Psychology*, 7, 13–21.

Littleton, K, Light, P, Joiner, R, Messer, D & Barnes, P (1992) Pairing and gender effects on children's computer-based learning. *European Journal of Psychology of Education*, 7, 311–324.

Locksley, A, Ortiz, V & Hepburn, C (1980) Social categorisation and discriminatory behaviour: extinguishing the minimal group discrimination effect. *Journal of Personality and Social Psychology*, 39, 773–783.

McAteer, E & Demissie, A (1991) *Writing Competence across the Curriculum*. Report to the Scottish Office Education Department.

McCaslin, M, Tuck, D, Wiard, A, Brown, B, Lapage, J & Pyle, J (1994) Gender composition and small-group learning in fourth grade mathematics. *Elementary School Journal*, 94, 467–482.

Morgan, V & Dunn, S (1988) Chameleons in the classroom: visible and invisible children in nursery and infant classrooms. *Educational Review*, 40, 3–12.

Newman, F & Holzman, L (1993) *Lev Vygotsky: Revolutionary Scientist.* Routledge.

Petersen, P, Johnson, D & Johnson, R (1991) Effects of co-operative learning on perceived status of male and female pupils. *Journal of Social Psychology*, 131, 717–735.

Plowden Report (1967) *Children and their Primary Schools.* Report of the Central Advisory Council for Education. HMSO.

Powney, J (1996) *Gender and Attainment: a Review.* SCRE Research Report 81. Edinburgh: The Scottish Council for Research in Education.

Pozzi, S, Healy, L & Hoyles, C (1993) Learning and interaction in groups with computers: when do ability and gender matter? *Social Development*, 2, 222–241.

Rennie, L J & Parker, L H (1987) Detecting and accounting for gender differences in mixed-sex and single-sex groupings in science lessons. *Educational Review*, 39, 65–73.

Rogoff, B (1992) *Apprenticeship in Thinking: Cognitive Development in Social Context.* New York: Oxford University Press.

Rutter, D (1989) An examination of teaching by telephone. In: Roger, D & Bull, P (eds) *Conversation: an Interdisciplinary Perspective.* Clevedon: Multilingual Matters.

Sadker, M & Sadker, D (1985) Sexism in the schoolroom of the 80's. *Psychology Today*, 54–57.

Siann, G & McLeod, H (1986) Computers and children of primary school age: issues and questions. *British Journal of Education Technology*, 2, 133–144.

Siann, G, McLeod, H, Glissov, P & Durndell, A (1990) The effect of computer use on gender differences in attitudes to computers. *Computers and Education*, 14, 183–191.

Simpson, A & Erickson, M (1983) Teachers' verbal and nonverbal communication patterns as a function of teacher race, student gender, and student race. *American Educational Research Journal*, 20, 183–198.

Sinclair, J McH & Coulthard, R M (1975) *Towards an Analysis of Discourse: The English used by Pupils and Teachers.* Oxford University Press.

Slavin, R E (1995) When and why does co-operative learning increase achievement? Theoretical and empirical perspectives. In: Hertz-

Lazarowitz, R & Miller, N (eds) *Interaction in Co-operative Groups: The Theoretical Anatomy of Group Learning.* Cambridge University Press.

Smith, A & Glynn, T (1990) Contexts for boys and girls learning mathematics: teacher interactions and student behaviour in two classrooms. *New Zealand Journal of Psychology*, 19, 9–16.

Smith, P, Howe, C J & Low, J (1995) Solving number problems: children working collaboratively. Paper presented at the BPS Developmental Section Conference, Strathclyde University.

SOED (1991) *English Language 5–14.* Edinburgh: HMSO.

SOED (1993) *Mathematics 5–14.* Edinburgh: HMSO.

Spender, D (1982) *Invisible Women: the Schooling Scandal.* Writers and Readers Publishing Cooperative.

Stake, J & Katz, J (1982) Teacher-pupil relationships in the elementary school classroom: teacher-gender and pupil-gender differences. *American Educational Research Journal*, 19, 465–471.

Stephenson, S (1994) The use of small groups in computer-based training: a review of recent literature. *Computers in Human Behavior*, 10, 243–259.

Swann, J (1992) *Girls, Boys and Language.* Oxford: Blackwell.

Swann, J & Graddol, D (1988) Gender inequalities in classroom talk. *English in Education*, 22, 48–65.

Taber, K S (1992) Girls' interactions with teachers in mixed physics classes – results of classroom observation. *International Journal of Science Education*, 14, 163-180.

Thompson, R B (1994) Gender differences in communicative style: possible consequences for the learning process. In: Foot, H C, Howe, C J, Anderson, A, Tolmie, A & Warden, D (eds) *Group and Interactive Learning.* Southampton: Computational Mechanics.

Tolmie, A & Howe, C J (1993) Gender and dialogue in secondary school physics. *Gender and Education*, 5, 191–209.

Tolmie, A, Howe, C J, Mackenzie, M & Greer, K (1993) Task design as an influence on dialogue and learning: primary school group work with object flotation. *Social Development*, 2, 183–201.

Underwood, G, Jindal, N & Underwood, J (1994) Gender differences and effects of co-operation in a computer-based language task. *Educational Research*, 36, 63–74.

Underwood, G, McCaffrey, M & Underwood, J (1990) Gender differences in a cooperative computer-based language task. *Educational Research, 32,* 44–49.

Underwood, G, Underwood, J & Turner, M (1993) Computer thinking during collaborative computer-based problem solving. *Educational Psychology, 13,* 345–357.

Wardhaugh, R (1992) *Sociolinguistics.* Oxford: Blackwell.

Wareing, S (1994) Gender, speech styles and the assessment of discussion. Unpublished PhD Dissertation, University of Strathclyde.

Webb, M (1989) Sex and gender in the labour market. In: Reid, I & Stratta, E (eds) *Sex Differences in Britain.* Aldershot: Gower.

Webb, N (1984) Sex differences in interaction and achievement in cooperative small groups. *Journal of Educational Psychology, 76,* 33–44.

Webb, N (1989) Peer interaction and learning in small groups. *International Journal of Educational Research, 13,* 21–39.

Whyte, J (1984) Observing sex stereotypes and interactions in the school lab and workshop. *Educational Review, 36,* 75–86.

Woods, N (1989) Talking shop: sex and status as determinants of floor apportionment in a work setting. In: Coates, J & Cameron, D (eds) *Women in their Speech Communities.* Longman.

Yelland, N J (1994) The strategies and interactions of young children in LOGO tasks. *Journal of Computer Assisted Learning, 10,* 33–49.

Zimmerman, D H & West, C (1975) Sex roles, interruptions and silences in conversation. In: Thorne, B & Henley, N (eds) *Language and Sex: Difference and Dominance.* Rowley, Mass: Newbury House.